Fun Facts & Trivia
1942 - A Year In Review

ISBN: 9798713680572

 INDEX

FIRST EDITION

1942

January

S	M	T	W	T	F	S
				1	2	3
4	5	6	7	8	9	10
11	12	13	14	15	16	17
18	19	20	21	22	23	24
25	26	27	28	29	30	31

○:2 ◐:10 ●:16 ◑:24

February

S	M	T	W	T	F	S
1	2	3	4	5	6	7
8	9	10	11	12	13	14
15	16	17	18	19	20	21
22	23	24	25	26	27	28

○:1 ◐:8 ●:15 ◑:22

March

S	M	T	W	T	F	S
1	2	3	4	5	6	7
8	9	10	11	12	13	14
15	16	17	18	19	20	21
22	23	24	25	26	27	28
29	30	31				

○:2 ◐:9 ●:16 ◑:24

April

S	M	T	W	T	F	S
			1	2	3	4
5	6	7	8	9	10	11
12	13	14	15	16	17	18
19	20	21	22	23	24	25
26	27	28	29	30		

○:1 ◐:8 ●:15 ◑:23 ○:30

May

S	M	T	W	T	F	S
					1	2
3	4	5	6	7	8	9
10	11	12	13	14	15	16
17	18	19	20	21	22	23
24	25	26	27	28	29	30
31						

◐:7 ●:15 ◑:23 ○:30

June

S	M	T	W	T	F	S
	1	2	3	4	5	6
7	8	9	10	11	12	13
14	15	16	17	18	19	20
21	22	23	24	25	26	27
28	29	30				

◐:5 ●:13 ◑:21 ○:28

July

S	M	T	W	T	F	S
			1	2	3	4
5	6	7	8	9	10	11
12	13	14	15	16	17	18
19	20	21	22	23	24	25
26	27	28	29	30	31	

◐:5 ●:13 ◑:21 ○:27

August

S	M	T	W	T	F	S
						1
2	3	4	5	6	7	8
9	10	11	12	13	14	15
16	17	18	19	20	21	22
23	24	25	26	27	28	29
30	31					

◐:3 ●:11 ◑:19 ○:25

September

S	M	T	W	T	F	S
		1	2	3	4	5
6	7	8	9	10	11	12
13	14	15	16	17	18	19
20	21	22	23	24	25	26
27	28	29	30			

◐:2 ●:10 ◑:17 ○:24

October

S	M	T	W	T	F	S
				1	2	3
4	5	6	7	8	9	10
11	12	13	14	15	16	17
18	19	20	21	22	23	24
25	26	27	28	29	30	31

◐:2 ●:10 ◑:16 ○:24

November

S	M	T	W	T	F	S
1	2	3	4	5	6	7
8	9	10	11	12	13	14
15	16	17	18	19	20	21
22	23	24	25	26	27	28
29	30					

◐:1 ●:8 ◑:15 ○:22 ◐:30

December

S	M	T	W	T	F	S
		1	2	3	4	5
6	7	8	9	10	11	12
13	14	15	16	17	18	19
20	21	22	23	24	25	26
27	28	29	30	31		

●:7 ◐:14 ○:22 ◑:30

PEOPLE IN HIGH OFFICE

Franklin D. Roosevelt
President - Democratic Party
March 4, 1933 - April 12, 1945

Born January 30, 1882, and commonly known by his initials FDR, he served as the 32nd President of the United States until his death on April 12, 1945.

77th United States Congress

Vice President	Henry A. Wallace
Chief Justice	Harlan F. Stone
Speaker of the House	Sam Rayburn
Senate Majority Leader	Alben W. Barkley

1942 U.S. Flag - 48 stars (1912-1959)

United Kingdom

King George VI
Dec 11, 1936 - Feb 6, 1952

Prime Minister
Winston Churchill
Conservative Party
May 10, 1940 - Jul 26, 1945

Australia

Prime Minister
John Curtin
Australian Labor Party
Oct 7, 1941
- Jul 5, 1945

Canada

Prime Minister
Mackenzie King
Liberal Party
Oct 23, 1935
- Nov 15, 1948

Ireland

Taoiseach of Ireland
Éamon de Valera
Fianna Fáil
Dec 29, 1937
- Feb 18, 1948

Argentina	**President** Roberto María Ortiz (1938-1942) Ramón Castillo (1942-1943)
Brazil	**President** Getúlio Vargas (1930-1945)
China	**Premier** Chiang Kai-shek (1939-1945)
Cuba	**President** Fulgencio Batista (1940-1944)
Egypt	**Prime Minister** Hussein Sirri Pasha (1940-1942) Mustafa el-Nahhas Pasha (1942-1944)
France	**President** *Vacant (1940-1944)*
Germany	**Chancellor** Adolf Hitler (1933-1945)
India	**Viceroy of India** Victor Alexander John Hope (1936-1943)

Italy	**Prime Minister** Benito Mussolini (1922-1943)
Japan	**Prime Minister** Hideki Tōjō (1941-1944)
Mexico	**President** LáManuel Ávila Camacho (1940-1946)
New Zealand	**Prime Minister** Peter Fraser (1940-1949)
Russia	**Communist Party Leader** Joseph Stalin (1922-1952)
South Africa	**Prime Minister** Jan Smuts (1939-1948)
Spain	**Prime Minister** Francisco Franco (1938-1973)
Turkey	**Prime Minister** Refik Saydam (1939-1942) Ahmet Fikri Tüzer (1942) Şükrü Saracoğlu (1942-1946)

AMERICAN NEWS & EVENTS

JAN

	President Franklin D. Roosevelt establishes the Joint Chiefs of Staff (JCS) to deal with the growing emergency arising from the recent Japanese attack on Pearl Harbor.
1	Sales of new 1942 model vehicles are frozen by the government's Office of Production Management (except for purchases by government agencies); estimates leave automobile manufacturers sitting on $175 million in unused inventory. *Follow up: By early February 1942 automobile factories had completely stopped manufacturing civilian vehicles and converted to producing tanks, aircraft, weapons, and other military products.*
2	The Navy opens a blimp base at Lakehurst, New Jersey.
4	The 1942 NFL All Star Game is held at the Polo Grounds in New York City and sees the Chicago Bears beat NFL All-Stars 35-24 in front of 17,725 spectators.
4	Rogers Hornsby becomes the 14th player elected to the Baseball Hall of Fame.

January 6: Pan American Airlines becomes the first commercial airline to schedule a flight around the world. The "Pacific Clipper", a Boeing 314 Clipper flying boat, completed its circumnavigation of the world when it landed at LaGuardia Field seaplane base in New York City after departing San Francisco on December 2, 1941. *Notes: One of the largest aircraft of its time, just twelve Boeing 314 Clippers (pictured) were built, nine of which served with Pan Am.*

7	United States and Philippine troops, under the command of General Douglas MacArthur, engage the Japanese in the Battle of Bataan. The battle lasts until April 9 and represents the most intense phase of the Japanese invasion of the Philippines during World War II.

January 9: In his 20th title defense Joe Louis KOs Buddy Baer in the 1st round of their rematch to retain his world heavyweight boxing titles at New York's Madison Square Garden (raising $47,000 for the Navy Relief Society). The next day he volunteers to enlist as a private in the Army at Camp Upton, Long Island. *Fun facts: In all, Louis made 25 defenses of his heavyweight titles from 1937 through 1948, and was a world champion for 11 years and 10 months. His most remarkable record is that he knocked out 23 opponents in 27 title fights, including five world champions. Photos: Private Joe Louis at Fort Dix (1942) / Joe Louis (1946).*

12	The National War Labor Board is established by President Roosevelt under Executive Order 9017 to mediate labor disputes during World War II.
13	Henry Ford patents a method for constructing auto bodies made out of plastic formed from soybeans. *Follow up: The plastic Ford was never made due to World War II and car production being halted.*
14	Operation Drumbeat: The German submarine U-123, under the command of Reinhard Hardegen, sinks the 9,500-ton Norwegian tanker Norness within sight of Long Island. No warships are dispatched to investigate and over the following nights U-123 is presented with a succession of easy targets including (the following night) the 6,700-ton British tanker Coimbra off Sandy Hook. *Notes: During the war U-123 conducted 12 war patrols, sinking 45 ships totalling 227,174-tons and damaging six others totaling 53,568-tons.*
15	President Roosevelt sends his famed "Green Light Letter" to MLB Commissioner Judge Landis encouraging baseball to continue to be played despite being at war.
16	Leading Danish-American automotive industry executive William Knudsen becomes the first civilian appointed a general in U.S. Army.
16	Actress Carole Lombard is among 22 killed aboard TWA Flight-3 after it crashed into Potosi Mountain near Las Vegas, Nevada. *NB: Lombard had been returning from a War Bond rally and had raised more than $2 million in defense bonds in a single evening. The crash was attributed to the flight crew's inability to properly navigate the mountains surrounding Las Vegas.*

17	The temperature at Richmond in Washington County, Rhode Island, drops to an all-time low of -28°F (state record).
19	VIII Bomber Command, later to become the Eighth Air Force, is established.
20	The Chicago Cubs drop plans to install lights at Wrigley Field because of military's need for materials. *Fun fact: Lights would finally be installed at the ballpark some 46 years later on August 8, 1988.*
25	The Japanese puppet state Thailand declares war on the United States and the United Kingdom.
26	The first American troops to enter the European Theatre of Operations land at Dufferin Dock in Belfast, Northern Ireland. *Interesting facts: Between 1942 and the end of the second world war around 300,000 American service personnel passed through Ulster. At its peak, U.S. military personnel made up around a tenth of Northern Ireland's population, and by the end of the war almost 2,000 women from Ulster had become GI brides.*

FEB

7	President Roosevelt signs an Executive Order 9054 creating the War Shipping Administration (WSA).
9	Daylight saving time goes into effect in the United States and is observed without disruption until September 30, 1945.

February 9: The seized ocean liner SS Normandie catches fire while being converted into the troopship USS Lafayette at pier 88 in New York City; hours later she capsizes. *Follow up: Although the French built ocean liner was salvaged and righted at great expense on August 7, 1943, restoration was deemed too costly and she was scrapped on October 3, 1946, without having ever sailed under the U.S. flag. Photo: A Coast Guard Grumman Widgeon aircraft flies over the wreck of Lafayette (1943).*

9	The Combined Chiefs of Staff (the supreme military staff for the United States and Britain during World War II) holds its first formal meeting to coordinate U.S. military operations between War and Navy Departments.
10	The record label RCA Victor presents Glenn Miller with the first ever gold record for selling a million copies of his hit recording "Chattanooga Choo Choo". The song, about a train ride from New York to Chattanooga in Tennessee, had been recorded on May 7, 1941, and when released had become an immediate success. *Fun fact: The 1941 recording of "Chattanooga Choo Choo" by Glenn Miller and His Orchestra was inducted into the Grammy Hall of Fame in 1996.*
11	The first issue of the comic book Archie, featuring Riverdale high-schooler Archie Andrews, is published.
18	Over 200 American sailors die off Newfoundland, Canada, after USS Truxtun and USS Pollux are grounded during a storm.
19	President Roosevelt signs Executive Order 9066 authorizing military commanders to designate "military areas" at their discretion "from which any or all persons may be excluded." *Follow up: These zones would result in the forced relocation and incarceration in concentration camps of thousands of people of Japanese, German and Italian ancestry, many of whom are American citizens.*
19	The New York Yankees announce that 5,000 uniformed soldiers will be admitted free at each of their upcoming home games.
19	Wild Bill Longson beats Sandor Szabo to become the NWA World Heavyweight wrestling champion.
20	Lieutenant Edward O'Hare becomes America's first World War II flying ace after he single-handedly attacks a formation of nine Japanese heavy bombers approaching his aircraft carrier. Even though he had a limited amount of ammunition he was credited with shooting down five of the enemy bombers and became the first naval recipient of the Medal of Honor in World War II. *Fun facts: On September 19, 1949, the Chicago-area Orchard Depot Airport was renamed O'Hare International Airport in his honor. Today it is the world's sixth-busiest airport, serving 83 million passengers in 2018.*
21	The U.S. male Figure Skating championship is won by Bobby Specht, and the female championship by Jane Vaughn Sullivan.
23	The Japanese submarine I-17 fires 17 high-explosive shells toward an oil refinery near Santa Barbara, California, causing little damage. *NB: The I-17 was the first Axis ship to shell the United States mainland.*
24	Battle of Los Angeles: Naval Intelligence issues a warning that an attack on mainland California could be expected within ten hours. In the early hours of February 25, air raid sirens sound throughout Los Angeles County and a total blackout is ordered. Shortly after over 1,400 anti-aircraft shells are fired at an unidentified, slow-moving object in the skies over Los Angeles. The "all clear" is sounded and the blackout order lifted at 7:21am. *Follow up: Within hours of the end of the air raid, Secretary of the Navy Frank Knox held a press conference saying the entire incident had been a false alarm due to anxiety and "war nerves" - several buildings and vehicles had been damaged by shell fragments, and five civilians had died as an indirect result of the anti-aircraft fire. In 1983, the Office of Air Force History concluded that an analysis of the evidence pointed to meteorological balloons as the cause of the initial alarm.*

February 26: The 14th Academy Awards ceremony, honoring the best in film for 1941, is held at the Biltmore Hotel in Los Angeles. The Oscar winners include John Ford's film How Green Was My Valley, Gary Cooper and Joan Fontaine. *NB: The ceremony is now considered notable, in retrospect, as the year in which Citizen Kane failed to win Best Picture (often later designated as the greatest film ever made). Photo: Gary Cooper, Joan Fontaine, and best supporting actors, Mary Astor and Donald Crisp.*

27	Battle of Java Sea: Allied navies suffer a disastrous defeat over a period of three days at the hands of the Imperial Japanese Navy. The defeat leads to the Japanese occupation of the entire Dutch East Indies.
28	Executive Order 9082 (February 28, 1942) reorganizes the United States Army into three major commands: Army Ground Forces, Army Air Forces, and Services of Supply (later redesignated Army Service Forces).

MAR

	Construction begins on the Badger Army Ammunition Plant near Baraboo, Wisconsin.
7	The first class of African-American pilots at Tuskegee Army Airfield in Macon County, Alabama, graduate after completing their advanced pilot training.
9	Construction of the Alaska Highway begins.
11	President Roosevelt orders General Douglas MacArthur to leave the Philippine island of Corregidor to go to Australia as American defense of the island (surrounded by the Japanese) collapses.
13	Julia O. Flikke of the Nurse Corps becomes the first woman to hold the rank of Colonel in the Army.
17	General MacArthur arrives in Melbourne, Australia, and is formally appointed supreme commander of the South-West Pacific Area.

MAR

18	President Roosevelt signs Executive Order 9102, creating the War Relocation Authority which is charged with overseeing the internment of Japanese Americans.
18	Black baseball players Jackie Robinson and Nate Moreland request a tryout with the Chicago White Sox. Manager Jimmy Dykes allows the two to practice with the team and has nothing but praise for both Robinson and Moreland. Dykes unfortunately had to turn both players down and the color barrier remains in effect. *Follow up: Robinson officially broke the major league color line when he put on a Dodgers uniform in front of 26,623 fans at Ebbets field on April 15, 1947.*
19	The Thoroughbred Racing Association is formed in Chicago with John C. Clark as president.
26	Hundreds of pounds of dynamite explode prematurely at a limestone quarry four miles north of Easton, Pennsylvania, killing 31 men.
27	In his 21st title defence (a military charity bout) Joe Louis KOs Abe Simon in the 6th round to retain his world heavyweight boxing titles at New York's Madison Square Garden; the fight nets $36,146.
28	In the 4th NCAA Men's Basketball Championship Stanford beats Dartmouth, 53-38; Cardinal forward Howie Dallmar is named the tournament's Most Outstanding Player.

APR

2	USS Hornet, under the command of Lieutenant Colonel Jimmy Doolittle, departs from San Francisco; their mission, a bombing raid on Japan.
9	After a three month fight American and Filipino forces surrender to the Japanese at Bataan. *Note: The surrender of the 76,000 troops at Bataan is the largest in United States military history since the American Civil War's Battle of Harper's Ferry.*
13	Byron Nelson wins the 9th Masters Tournament at Augusta National Golf Club in Augusta, Georgia.
14	The destroyer USS Roper sinks the German submarine U-85 off Bodie Island on the Outer Banks, North Carolina. Numerous men are observed in the water but no rescue attempt is made until daylight - by then there were no survivors among the 29 bodies floating in life jackets.
18	The American task force on its way to Japan, which includes USS Hornet, is spotted by a Japanese patrol boat. Lieutenant Colonel Doolittle and his 16 B-25 raiders launch prematurely (from 690 miles out instead of the planned 460 miles), reach Japan and bomb their targets. *Follow up: Due to lack of fuel none of the 16 planes made it to their designated landing strips in China. Fifteen aircraft reached China but all crashed, while the 16th landed at Vladivostok in the Soviet Union. Of the 80 crew members, 77 survived the mission. Eight airmen were captured by Imperial Japanese Army troops in Eastern China; three were later executed. Doolittle initially believed that the loss of all his aircraft would lead to his court-martial, but he instead received the Medal of Honor and was promoted two ranks to Brigadier General.*
18	The Toronto Maple Leafs beat Detroit Red Wings, 3-1 for a 4-3 series win in Stanley Cup Final at Maple Leaf Gardens in Toronto.
20	Joe Smith wins the 46th Boston Marathon in a course record time of 2:26:51.

April 27: A tornado sweeps along Pryor Creek's main street in Mayes County, Oklahoma, destroying nearly every building from the western edge of the business district to the eastern edge of the city. The Associated Press reports two days later that 60 people have been killed in the storm and around 400 injured; the damaged caused is estimated at US$3 million. *Pictured: Pryor main street after the tornado.*

30	The first freshwater built submarine, SS-265 USS Peto, is launched on Lake Michigan in the port city of Manitowoc, Wisconsin.

MAY

2	The 68th Kentucky Derby sees jockey Wayne D. Wright win aboard Shut Out.
4	The Battle of Coral Sea begins. *NB: The battle is historically significant as the first naval battle fought solely in air (between the Imperial Japanese Navy and naval and air forces of the United States and Australia).*
4	The Pulitzer Prize for the Novel (now the Pulitzer Prize for Fiction) is awarded to Ellen Glasgow for In This Our Life.
5	Sugar becomes the first consumer commodity rationed in United States; people are limited to ½ pound per person per week.
6	In the Philippines the Battle of Corregidor ends as the last American and Filipino forces surrender to the Japanese.
8	At Ebbets Field the first twilight game in 24 years sees the Dodgers beat the Giants 7-6, raising $59,859 for the Navy Relief Fund.
12	German submarine U-507 sinks the oil tanker SS Virginia anchored off the mouth of the Mississippi River in the Gulf of Mexico; 26 of the 40 crew are lost.
14	Aaron Copland's "A Lincoln Portrait" is performed for the first time by the Cincinnati Symphony Orchestra, with William Adams as the narrator.
15	The creation of the Women's Auxiliary Army Corps (WAAC) is signed into law. President Roosevelt sets a recruitment goal of 25,000 women for the first year.
15	Gasoline rationing begins in 17 Eastern States.

22	Future baseball Hall of Famer and Boston Red Sox star Ted Williams enlists as a Navy aviator.
27	Admiral Chester W. Nimitz awards Doris "Dorie" Miller the Navy Cross for distinguished devotion to duty, extraordinary courage and disregard for his own personal safety during the attack on the Fleet in Pearl Harbor; Miller is the first black American to be awarded the Navy Cross.
29	Bing Crosby records White Christmas for Decca Records with the John Scott Trotter Orchestra and the Ken Darby Singers. *Fun facts: Written by Irving Berlin for the musical film Holiday Inn (1942), White Christmas is the world's best-selling single of all time with estimated sales in excess of 50 million copies worldwide. The composition also notably won the Academy Award for Best Original Song at the 15th Academy Awards on March 4, 1943.*
29	The movie Yankee Doodle Dandy, based on life of George M. Cohan and starring James Cagney and Joan Lesley, premieres in New York. The film is a major hit for Warner Brothers and is nominated for eight Academy Awards (winning three).
31	Sam Snead wins the 25th PGA Golf Championship at Seaview Country Club in Galloway Township, New Jersey.

June 4-7: Battle of Midway: Six months after Japan's attack on Pearl Harbor and one month after the Battle of the Coral Sea, the U.S. Navy under Admirals Chester W. Nimitz, Frank J. Fletcher, and Raymond A. Spruance, defeat an attacking fleet of the Imperial Japanese Navy near Midway Atoll. The devastating damage inflicted during the battle (which renders the Japanese aircraft carriers irreparable) has been described as the most stunning and decisive blow in the history of naval warfare. *Photo: Smoke pours from USS Yorktown after being hit by Japanese dive bombers at Midway.*

| 4 | The patriotic Academy Award-winning drama film Mrs Miniver, starring Greer Garson and Walter Pidgeon, premieres in New York. |

JUN

5	The United States Congress declares war on Bulgaria, Hungary and Romania.
5	An explosion at the Joliet Army Ammunition Plant in Will County, Illinois, kills 48 people.
6	The Garden State Park horse racetrack opens for business (the first licensed New Jersey racetrack). Despite the rainy weather 31,682 race fans turn up and bet a total of $569,341 on the days eight races.
7	The crippled aircraft carrier USS Yorktown is sunk near Midway after being hit by a salvo of torpedoes fired from the Japanese submarine I-168.
6	Japanese forces invade Alaska's Aleutian Islands, Kiska and Attu (June 7), to the shock of the American public; it is the first time since the War of 1812 that the continental United States has been invaded.
13	The Office of War Information opens with journalist and CBS newsman Elmer Davis as its head.
18	Bernard W. Robinson becomes the first African-American Naval officer commissioned in the U.S. Naval Reserve.
21	Fort Stevens, Oregon, is fired upon by a Japanese submarine I-25.
25	Dwight D. Eisenhower is appointed commander of U.S. forces in Europe.
27	Two groups of four Nazi saboteurs, who had landed by submarine off New York and Florida either in the month, are captured by the FBI. Apprehended without having accomplished any acts of destruction, they are tried before a military commission and found guilty. One is sentenced to life imprisonment, another to 30 years, and six receive the death penalty, which is carried out within a few days.

JUL

4	The U.S. Eighth Air Force flies its first inauspicious mission in Europe using borrowed British planes to attack the Dutch Alkmaar, Hammsted, and Valkenburg airfields; of the six aircraft that went out only three make it back.
4	Irving Berlin's musical "This is the Army" premieres on Broadway. Designed to boost war time morale in the United States, it is produced by the Army (with a cast of soldiers) for the benefit of the Army Emergency Relief Fund.
17	An estimated 34.5" of rain falls in 12 hours near Smethport, Pennsylvania. *NB: The National Climatic Data Center (NCDC) claims this is "arguably the greatest 24-hour rainfall on record outside of the tropics".*
20	The first detachment of the Women's Army Auxiliary Corps begins basic training at Fort Des Moines, Iowa.
20	The Legion of Merit Medal is authorized by Congress.
30	A bill officially establishing the United States Marine Corps Women's Reserve (USMCWR) and the Women Accepted for Volunteer Emergency Service (WAVES) is authorized by Congress and signed into law by President Roosevelt.

AUG

7	The Battle of Guadalcanal, the first major land offensive by Allied forces against the Empire of Japan, begins (ends February 9, 1943). *NB: The Guadalcanal campaign is widely considered, along with the Battle of Midway, a turning point in the Pacific War.*

9	CBS radio broadcasts the debut of "Our Secret Weapon." *Notes: Created to counter Axis shortwave radio propaganda broadcasts during World War II, writer Rex Stout (chairman of the Writers' War Board) would rebut the most entertaining lies of the week.*
13	The 'Manhattan Project' is officially created under the direction of Major General Leslie Groves of the Army Corps of Engineers (its aim is to deliver an atomic bomb).
13	Walt Disney's fifth animated movie Bambi, based on the book "Bambi, a Life in the Woods" by Austrian author Felix Salten, premieres in New York.
14	The USAAF down their first German warplane, a Focke-Wulf Fw 200 Condor, off the coast of Reykjavík, Iceland.
15	Operation Pedestal: The American tanker SS Ohio reaches Malta as part of a British operation to carry vital supplies to the island.

August 16: The Navy Blimp L-8, on an anti-submarine patrol flight, drifts ashore near San Francisco at Daly City. Mysteriously neither of the crewmen, Lt. E. D. Cody and Ensign C. Adams, are onboard; no trace of either man has ever been found. *Photo: The Blimp L-8 (of Blimp Squadron ZP-32), her gondola empty and door locked open, finally comes to rest on Bellevue Ave at the base of Mount San Bruno in Daly City.*

17	Eighth Air Force bombers (escorted by British RAF Spitfires) bomb the Sotteville railyard 3 miles South of Rouen, France. It is the "first combat action" of the Eighth Air Force, and the first B-17 bombing of Europe.
23	55-year-old Walter Johnson pitches to 48-year-old Babe Ruth for one last time in between games of a doubleheader at Yankee Stadium. The face off, watched by 69,000 fans, helps raise $80,000 for the Army-Navy Service Fund.

SEP

7	The Consolidated B-32 Dominator strategic bomber makes its first flight.

SEP

9 A Yokosuka E14Y floatplane, flown by Japanese pilot Nobuo Fujita, is launched from the long-range submarine aircraft carrier I-25 from which it executes the first-ever bombing of the continental United States by an enemy aircraft. Its mission to start massive forest fires in the Pacific Northwest near the city of Brookings, Oregon, fails to have its desired effect thanks to light winds and a quick response from fire patrols. *Follow up: After the war pilot Nobuo Fujita visited Brooking a number of times, donating his family's 400-year-old katana in friendship and planting a tree at the bomb site as a gesture of peace. Several days before his death at the age of 85 he was made an honorary citizen of Brookings. His daughter, Yoriko Asakura, later buried some of his ashes at the bomb site.*

OCT

1 The Bell P-59 Airacomet, the first jet-engined fighter produced in the United States, makes its maiden flight. *NB: Although no P-59s entered combat, the aircraft paved the way for later generations of American turbojet-powered aircraft.*

3 The Office of Economic Stabilization is established as a means to control wartime inflation (through regulations on price, wage, and salary increases).

3 1941 Triple Crown winner Whirlaway, ridden by George Woolf, wins the Jockey Club Gold Cup at Belmont Park to become the first thoroughbred to amass more than $500,000 in lifetime earnings.

5 The St. Louis Cardinals defeat the New York Yankees 4 games to 1 to win their fourth World Series title.

7 French Canadian Yvon Robert beats Bill Longson in Montreal, Quebec, to become the NWA World Heavyweight wrestling champion.

October 8: The Comedy duo Abbott and Costello relaunch their NBC weekly radio show after a hiatus of two years; the program runs until June 9, 1949.

| 23 | All 12 passengers and crewmen aboard American Airlines Flight 28 are killed when it is struck by an Army Air Force bomber near Palm Springs, California. Amongst the victims is the award-winning composer and Hollywood songwriter Ralph Rainger (Academy Award for Best Original Song 1938 – "Thanks for the Memory"). |
| 25 | Battle of the Santa Cruz Islands: A Japanese naval offensive against U.S. forces near the Solomon Islands results in two Japanese aircraft carriers being heavily damaged and one U.S. carrier sunk. It is the fourth major naval engagement fought between the U.S. Navy and the Imperial Japanese Navy during the lengthy and strategically important Guadalcanal campaign. |

VIEW ALONG THE NEW ALASKA HIGHWAY THROUGH CANADA'S WILDERNESS
BUILT BY A WELCOME ARMY OF U. S. SOLDIERS
PERMISSION WARTIME INFORMATION BOARD

October 28: The Alaska Highway is completed with the northern linkup at Mile 1202, Beaver Creek. *Interesting facts: The Alaska Highway, dedicated on November 20, 1942, at Soldier's Summit, was built (mostly) by 10,000 men of the U.S. Army Corps of Engineers as a supply route. Although completed in 1942 it was not usable by general vehicles until 1943, and wasn't opened to the public until 1948. When built the highway was about 1,680 miles in length, running from Dawson Creek, British Columbia, to Delta Junction, Alaska. Today it is just 1,387 miles in length due to the continuing reconstruction of the highway (which has rerouted and straightened many sections). Photo: Postcard of Suicide Hill on the Alcan Highway, Mile 148 (circa 1942).*

| 28 | A Grand Trunk Western railroad passenger train strikes a school bus in Detroit Michigan, killing 16 and injuring 20. |
| 29 | Branch Rickey is named president and General Manager of the Brooklyn Dodgers; Rickey was instrumental in breaking baseball's color barrier when he signed Jackie Robinson for the Dodgers in 1947. |

NOV

	John H. Johnson publishes the first issue of Negro Digest in Chicago, Illinois. The magazine, similar to the Reader's Digest, aims to cover positive stories about the African-American community.
3	Boston Red Sox outfielder Ted Williams wins the American League Triple Crown (36 HRs, 137 RBI, .356 average), but New York Yankees pitcher Joe Gordon is named AL MVP.
8	British and American troops, commanded by General Dwight D. Eisenhower, invade French North Africa in Operation Torch. It is the first mass involvement of U.S. troops in the European-North African Theatre, and sees the first major airborne assault carried out by the United States.
9	American soldier and serial killer Edward Leonski is hanged at Pentridge Prison for the "Brown-Out" murders of three women in Melbourne, Australia. *Note: Leonski is the first and only citizen of another country to have been tried and sentenced to death in Australia under the law of his own country.*
11	Congress votes to amend the Selective Service Act of 1940, lowering the draft age to 18 and raising the upper limit to age 37.
12	A four-day naval battle near Guadalcanal begins between Japanese and American forces; both sides lose numerous warships in two extremely destructive surface engagements. *Follow up: The battle turned back Japan's last major attempt to dislodge Allied forces from Guadalcanal (and nearby Tulagi) resulting in a strategic victory for the U.S. and its allies.*
23	A bill creating the United States Coast Guard Women's Reserve (SPARS) is signed into law by President Roosevelt.
26	The movie Casablanca, starring Humphrey Bogart and Ingrid Bergman, premieres at the Hollywood Theater in New York City (Academy Awards Best Picture 1943).
27	Bobby Managoff beats Yvon Robert in Houston, Texas, to become the NWA World Heavyweight wrestling champion.
28	A fire at the Cocoanut Grove nightclub in Boston, Massachusetts, kills 492 people. *NB: The fire (the deadliest nightclub fire in history) leads to a reform of safety standards and codes across America.*
29	Coffee rationing begins across the U.S. limiting people to one pound every five weeks (in part because of German U-boat attacks on shipping from Brazil).

DEC

2	A team led by Enrico Fermi initiates the world's first self-sustaining nuclear chain reaction at the University of Chicago.
6	American B-24 Liberators out of North Africa strike the Italian mainland for first time leaving Naples harbor in ruins.
13	The Washington Redskins upset the Chicago Bears, 14-6, in the 10th NFL Championship Game at Griffith Stadium in Washington, D.C.
19	Robert Stroud (the Birdman of Alcatraz) is transferred to Alcatraz Federal Penitentiary (inmate No.594).
22	An avalanche kills 26 when 200 tons of rock and dirt smashes down on a bus filled with wartime steel workers and Christmas shoppers on their way home from Aliquippa to Ambridge Pennsylvania.
28	Captain Robert Sullivan, flying from New York to Portugal, becomes the first pilot to fly across the Atlantic 100 times.

Worldwide News & Events

1. January: The Mildenhall Treasure, a large hoard of 34 masterpieces of Roman silver tableware from the fourth century AD, is discovered by a ploughman near Mildenhall in Suffolk, England. *NB: The collection is on view today at the British Museum and is a permanent feature of the museum's Romano-British gallery.*

2. January 1: Representatives of 26 countries fighting the Rome-Berlin-Tokyo Axis decide to affirm their support by signing the Declaration of The United Nations. *Notes: President Roosevelt, British Prime Minister Winston Churchill, Maxim Litvinov of the USSR and T.V. Soong of China signed the short document on New Year's Day, followed on the 2nd January by the representatives of twenty-two other nations. The declaration pledged the signatory governments to the maximum war effort and bound them against making a separate peace.*

3. January 11: The Japanese conquer Kuala Lumpur in Malaya. They encounter very little resistance; British troops had already left the city.

4. January 13: German test pilot Helmut Schenk becomes the first person to escape from a stricken aircraft using an ejector seat at Rechlin in Germany.

5. January 20: Senior Nazi government officials and Schutzstaffel (SS) leaders hold the notorious Wannsee Conference in Berlin to organise the 'Final Solution to the Jewish Question', the rounding up and extermination of Europe's Jews.

6. January 27: A record low of -17.3°F (-27.4°C) is recorded by Jaap Langedijk in Dutch town of Winterswijk; it is the coldest day in the Netherlands since 1850.

7. February: British Army research officer James Stanley Hey becomes the first person to detect radio emissions from the Sun, laying the basis for the development of radio astronomy.

8. February 1: Vidkun Quisling is elected to the post of Minister-President of the Norwegian national government. *Follow up: Quisling, a Nazi collaborator, was executed by firing squad in Oslo on October 24, 1945 after being found guilty of charges including embezzlement, murder and high treason against the Norwegian state. The word "quisling" is now more commonly known for a person who collaborates with an enemy occupying force, a traitor.*

9. February 14: The Polish resistance movement, the Home Army, is formed. *Note: It will eventually become the largest resistance movement in occupied Europe.*

10. February 15: Lieutenant-General Arthur Ernest Percival's forces surrender to the Japanese at the Battle of Singapore. Around 80,000 British, Indian and Australian troops in Singapore become prisoners of war in what is the largest surrender of British-led forces in history.

11. February 16: Bangka Island Massacre: Japanese soldiers machine-gun 22 Australian Army nurses and 60 Australian and British soldiers who had survived the sinking of Vyner Brooke by Japanese bombers; only one nurse and two soldiers survive.

12. February 19: In the largest single attack ever mounted by a foreign power on Australia, the Japanese launch 242 warplanes (in two separate raids) attacking the city of Darwin.

13. March 5: The world premiere of Dmitri Shostakovich's 7th Symphony takes place in Kuybyshev (now Samara), Russia. *NB: The work is regarded as a major musical testament to the 27 million Soviet people who lost their lives in World War II, and it is often played at Leningrad Cemetery where half a million victims of the 900-day Siege of Leningrad are buried.*

14.	March 17: The Nazi extermination camp Bełżec begins the systematic gassing of Jews. *NB: Between 430,000 and 500,000 Jews are believed to have been murdered by the SS at Bełżec, making it the third-deadliest Nazi extermination camp, exceeded only by Treblinka and Auschwitz.*
15.	March 27: The first transport of French Jews to Auschwitz by Nazi-Germany takes place. *NB: Of the 75,721 deportees from France to Nazi extermination camps only 2,560 survived through to 1945.*
16.	March 28: Operation Chariot: A daring amphibious attack by the British Royal Navy and Commandos is undertaken on the heavily defended Normandie dry dock at St Nazaire in German-occupied France. *Follow up: The operation is a major tactical success and puts the dock out of service until 1948. Of the 611 men who took part in the raid, 169 were killed (German causalities were in excess of 360). To recognise their bravery 89 men were awarded decorations including five Victoria Crosses (Britain's highest and most prestigious award for valor).*
17.	April 15: King George VI awards the George Cross to people of Malta so as to "bear witness to the heroism and devotion of its people". *Fun fact: The George Cross was incorporated into the flag of Malta in 1943 and remains in the current design to this day.*

18. April 23: Exeter in England becomes the first city bombed by German Luftwaffe as part of the "Baedeker Blitz" in retaliation for the British bombing of Lübeck. *Notes: The Baedeker Blitz continued from late April through early June and was a tit-for-tat exchange by the Luftwaffe with the hope of forcing the RAF to reduce their attacks on Germany. Targets were chosen to increase the effect on civilian life, and for their cultural and historical significance, rather than for any military value. Photo: The bombed ruins of Southernhay West in Exeter after the Baedeker Raids in Spring 1942.*

19. April 25: Sixteen-year-old Princess Elizabeth (the only woman in the British royal family to have served in the military) registers for war service under the Ministry of Labour's Youth Registration Scheme. *Interesting facts: Princess Elizabeth became Queen Elizabeth II after the death of her father George VI on February 6, 1952. She surpassed her great-great-grandmother, Queen Victoria, to become the longest-lived British monarch on December 21, 2007, and became the longest-reigning queen regnant and female head of state in the world on September 9, 2015. Photos: Princess Elizabeth (truck mechanic No.230873) in her Auxiliary Territorial Service uniform in front of an Army ambulance during WWII / The Princess, wearing her Girl Guides uniform, signs up for war service.*

20.	April 26: A gas and coal-dust explosion kills 1,549 at the Honkeiko colliery in Liaoning, China (then part of the Japanese-controlled puppet state of Manchukuo). Although some workers are killed by the explosion an investigation after the war by the Soviet Union found that most deaths were from carbon monoxide poisoning (produced when the Japanese shut off the ventilation and sealed the pit in an attempt to curtail the fire). *Note: The Honkeiko colliery disaster is the worst in the history of coal mining.*
21.	April 29: Jewish Dutch people are ordered to wear yellow badges by the German authorities; Belgian Jews and Jews in occupied France are ordered to do the same on June 3, and June 7, respectively.
22.	May 12: David Ben-Gurion assembles an emergency conference of American Zionists in New York City; the convention decides upon the establishment of a Jewish commonwealth in Palestine after the war. *Notes: The State of Israel was established on May 14, 1948, with Ben-Gurion its primary national founder and first Prime Minister.*
23.	May 22: Mexican President Manuel Ávila Camacho issues a formal declaration of war against the Axis Powers after the sinking of two Mexican oil tankers by German U-boats.
24.	May 26: The Anglo-Soviet Treaty (establishing a military and political alliance between the Soviet Union and the British Empire) is signed in London by British Foreign Secretary Anthony Eden and Soviet Foreign Minister Vyacheslav Molotov.
25.	May 27: Nazi leader Reinhard Heydrich (one of the most powerful men in Nazi Germany and an important figure in the rise of Adolf Hitler) is mortally wounded by a grenade thrown by Czech rebels in Prague during Operation Anthropoid.

26.	May 30: Operation Millennium: The British RAF dispatches 1,047 bombers to Cologne in its first "thousand bomber raid". It is the largest bombing raid of World War II.
27.	June 12: In Amsterdam Anne Frank gets a diary for her 13th birthday; she begins writing in it two days later. *Notes: Published posthumously (she is believed to have died of typhus in the Bergen-Belsen concentration camp in February or March 1945) the "The Diary of a Young Girl" has received widespread critical and popular attention and been translated into over 70 languages.*
28.	June 18: Eric Nessler of France stays aloft in a glider for a record 38h:21m:24s over the Montagne Noire, in the Haute-Garonne, France.
29.	June 19: British Prime Minister Winston Churchill arrives in Washington, D.C. for a conference (June 19-25). An agreement is reached to start preparations for an invasion of the North African Colonies of Vichy France (Operation Torch).
30.	June 21: The highest temperature ever recorded in Asia, 129°F (54°C), is set at Tirat Zvi in Israel.
31.	June 21: The Axis forces, led by Generalleutnant Erwin Rommel, take Tobruk in North Africa.

32. June 23: German Luftwaffe pilot Armin Faber lands his Focke-Wulf FW190 (Germany's latest fighter aircraft) at Pembrey in Wales. Disoriented Faber had mistaken the Bristol Channel for the English Channel and thought he was landing in France. Observers on the ground could not believe their eyes as Faber waggled his wings in a victory celebration, before lowering the Focke-Wulf's undercarriage and landing. *Follow up: Faber's plane was the first FW190 to be captured by the Allies and this allowed it to be tested to reveal any weaknesses that could be exploited. Photo: Faber's captured Focke Wulf at the Royal Aircraft Establishment with the RAE's chief test pilot, Wing Commander H J "Willie" Wilson at the controls (August 1942).*

33.	June 30: For the second month in a row U-boats sink and damage 146 allied ships; these are the highest monthly totals recorded during WWII (May - 146 ships, 722,666-tons / June - 146 ships, 700,227-tons).
34.	July 18: The Messerschmitt Me 262 makes its first flight under jet power in Leipheim near Günzburg, Germany. Flown by test pilot Fritz Wendel, it is the world's first operational jet-powered fighter aircraft.

35.	July 22: Over a period of eight weeks Warsaw Ghetto inmates are shuttled by train to the Treblinka extermination camp. The operation, led by SS-Sturmbannführer Hermann Höfle, sees the murder of 254,000 Jews at the camp between July 23 and September 21.
36.	August 8: Lieutenant-General Bernard Montgomery is appointed commander of the British Eighth Army in North Africa.
37.	August 9: British officials imprison Mahatma Gandhi hoping to suppress a civil disobedience program intended to free India from colonial rule.
38.	August 12: Prime Minister Winston Churchill arrives in Moscow for a conference with Joseph Stalin and U.S. representative W. Averrell Harriman.
39.	August 19: Canadian and British troops conduct the Dieppe Raid (Operation Jubilee), an amphibious attack on the German-occupied port of Dieppe in northern France. Aerial and naval support is insufficient to enable the ground forces to achieve their objectives and within ten hours, of the 6,086 men who landed, 3,623 had been killed, wounded or become prisoners of war. *Follow up: The lessons of the Dieppe Raid influenced preparations for Allied seaborne operations in the Mediterranean and the Normandy landings (Operation Overlord).*
40.	August 22: Brazil, under the dictatorship of Getúlio Vargas, declares war on Germany, Japan and Italy.
41.	August 23: The Battle of Stalingrad: Germany and its allies begin their fight against the Soviet Union for control of the city of Stalingrad (now Volgograd) in Southern Russia. *Follow up: The battle, marked by fierce close-quarters combat and direct assaults on civilians in air raids, is one of the bloodiest battles in the history of warfare with an estimated 2 million casualties. The Axis forces, having exhausted their ammunition and food, surrendered on February 2, 1943.*
42.	September 20: Swedish runner Gunther Hagg sets a world record time in the 5000m (13m:58.2s) to become the World Record Holder at all distances from 1500m to 5000m.
43.	October 2: The Japanese troopship Lisbon Maru sinks following a torpedo attack the previous day by U.S. Navy submarine USS Grouper off the coast of China: 829 are killed, mostly British prisoners of war who (unknown to the attacker) are being held on board.
44.	October 3: The first V-2 rocket is successfully launched from Test Stand VII at Peenemünde in Germany; it flies a distance of 91.3 miles (147km) and reaches a height of 52.5 miles (84.5km). *Interesting facts: The V-2 rocket became the first artificial object to travel into space when crossing the Kármán line (measured at 62 miles (100km) above Earth's mean sea level) on June 20, 1944.*
45.	October 5: Oxfam: The first meeting of the Oxford Committee for Famine Relief (founded by a group of Quakers, social activists and Oxford academics) is held in the Old Library, the University Church, Oxford, England.
46.	October 9: The Statute of Westminster Adoption Act is passed by the Parliament of Australia formalising Australian autonomy from the United Kingdom.
47.	October 16: A Cyclone in Bay of Bengal, India, near the West Bengal / Odisha border, kills some 15,000 people.
48.	November 6: The German Luftwaffe Heinkel He 219 night fighter aircraft makes its first flight; it is the first operational military aircraft to be equipped with an ejector seat.
49.	November 7: Cyclist Fausto Coppi establishes a new world hour record of 45.798km/h in Milan, Italy.
50.	November 8: Adolf Hitler prematurely proclaims the fall of Stalingrad to senior members of the Nazi Party at the Löwenbräukeller (a beer hall) in Stiglmaierplatz, Munich.

51. November 11: Second Battle of El Alamein: Field Marshal Erwin Rommel is comprehensively defeated by the British Eighth Army under the command of Lieutenant-General Bernard Montgomery. The Allied victory is the beginning of the end of the Western Desert Campaign, eliminating the Axis threat to Egypt, the Suez Canal and the Middle Eastern and Persian oil fields. *Photos: Montgomery in the turret of his Grant command tank at El Alamein / British troops unloading fuel drums at El-Alamein during the North Africa campaigns.*

52.	November 23: Chinese sailor Poon Lim, working as second steward on the British merchant ship SS Benlomond, jumps overboard after the Benlomond is hit by torpedoes from German submarine U-172. The sole survivor, he finds an eight-foot wooden raft and begins what will be 133 days adrift in the South Atlantic. *Follow up: Lin was rescued by three fishermen as he neared the coast of Brazil on April 5, 1943. After four weeks in a Brazilian hospital the British Consul arranged for him to return to Britain. Upon his return Lin was awarded a British Empire Medal by King George VI. After the war, Lim emigrated to the United States.*
53.	November 26: The first operational military Bailey bridge is erected by British Royal Engineers over the Medjerda River near Medjez el Bab in Tunisia. *Interesting facts: Invented by Donald Bailey (a civil servant in the British War Office), by the end of the war the U.S. Fifth Army and British Eighth Army had built over 3,000 Bailey bridges in Sicily and Italy alone.*
54.	December 10: An official diplomatic note from the government of Poland in exile, regarding the extermination of Jews in German-occupied Poland, is sent to the foreign ministers of the Allies. It is the first official report on the Holocaust.
55.	December 24: The first powered flight of the V-1 flying bomb (aka; buzz bomb or doodlebug) takes place at Peenemunde in Germany. *Notes: An early cruise missile and the only production aircraft to use a pulsejet for power, the V-1 was the first of the so-called "Vengeance weapons" series (Vergeltungswaffen) deployed for the terror bombing of London, England.*
56.	December 31: The Battle of the Barents Sea takes place between warships of the German Navy (Kriegsmarine) and British ships escorting convoy JW 51B to Kola Inlet in the USSR. *Note: The German raiders' failure to inflict significant losses on the convoy infuriated Hitler who ordered that German naval strategy would henceforth concentrate on the U-boat fleet rather than surface ships.*

BIRTHS

American Personalities

BORN IN 1942

Donna Axum
b. January 3, 1942
d. November 4, 2018
Former Miss America, author, television producer, philanthropist and model.

Muhammad Ali
b. January 17, 1942
d. June 3, 2016
Professional boxer, activist, entertainer and philanthropist.

Edwin Starr
b. January 21, 1942
d. April 2, 2003
Singer and songwriter.

Steve Wynn
b. January 27, 1942

Businessman known for his involvement in the luxury casino and hotel industry.

John Witherspoon
b. January 27, 1942
d. October 29, 2019
Actor and comedian.

Roger Staubach
b. February 5, 1942

Hall of Fame professional football player.

Carole King
b. February 9, 1942

Singer-songwriter who has written (or co-written) 118 Billboard Hot 100 hits.

Peter Tork
b. February 13, 1942
d. February 21, 2019
Musician, composer and actor best known as a member of The Monkees.

Michael Bloomberg
b. February 14, 1942

Businessman, politician, philanthropist and author.

Mitch McConnell
b. February 20, 1942

Businessmen and Republican politician (Senate Majority Leader, 2015-2021).

30

Joe Lieberman
b. February 24, 1942

Politician, attorney and former Democratic
Party nominee for Vice President (2000).

Lou Reed
b. March 2, 1942
d. October 27, 2013
Musician, singer, songwriter and poet.

Aretha Franklin
b. March 25, 1942
d. August 16, 2018
Singer, songwriter, actress, pianist and civil
rights activist.

Jerry Sloan
b. March 28, 1942
d. May 22, 2020
Professional basketball player and
Basketball Hall of Fame coach.

Wayne Newton
b. April 3, 1942

Singer and actor who is one of the best-
known entertainers in Las Vegas.

Barbra Streisand
b. April 24, 1942

Multiple award winning singer, actress and
filmmaker.

31

Tammy Wynette

b. May 5, 1942
d. April 6, 1998

Country music singer-songwriter and musician.

Curtis Mayfield

b. June 3, 1942
d. December 26, 1999

Singer-songwriter, guitarist and record producer.

Roger Ebert

b. June 18, 1942
d. April 4, 2013

Film critic, film historian, journalist, screenwriter and author.

Brian Wilson

b. June 20, 1942

Musician, singer, songwriter and record producer (co-founder of the Beach Boys).

Michele Lee

b. June 24, 1942

Actress, singer, dancer, producer and director.

Willis Reed

b. June 25, 1942

Hall of Fame basketball player, coach and general manager.

Bruce Johnston
b. June 27, 1942

Singer, songwriter and record producer
(Beach Boys).

Frank Zane
b. June 28, 1942

Professional bodybuilder and author who
was a three-time Mr. Olympia.

Ronnie James Dio
b. July 10, 1942
d. May 16, 2010

Heavy metal singer-songwriter and
composer.

Harrison Ford
b. July 13, 1942

Actor, pilot and environmental activist.

Roger McGuinn
b. July 13, 1942

Musician best known for being the frontman
and leader of The Byrds.

Connie Hawkins
b. July 17, 1942
d. October 6, 2017

Hall of Fame basketball player.

Jerry Garcia

b. August 1, 1942
d. August 9, 1995
Singer-songwriter and guitarist with the rock band the Grateful Dead.

Al Jardine

b. September 3, 1942

Musician, singer and songwriter (co-founder of the Beach Boys).

Frankie Lymon

b. September 30, 1942
d. February 27, 1968
Rock and roll / rhythm and blues singer and songwriter (The Teenagers).

Joy Behar

b. October 7, 1942

Comedian, television host, actress and writer.

Melvin Franklin

b. October 12, 1942
d. February 23, 1995
Bass singer and founding member of Motown singing group The Temptations.

Judy Sheindlin

b. October 21, 1942

Lawyer, former family court judge, television personality, producer and author.

Annette Funicello
b. October 22, 1942
d. April 8, 2013
Actress, singer and one of the original
Mouseketeers.

Michael Crichton
b. October 23, 1942
d. November 4, 2008
Author and filmmaker whose books have
sold over 200 million copies worldwide.

Bob Ross
b. October 29, 1942
d. July 4, 1995
Painter, art instructor and television host
(The Joy of Painting).

Stefanie Powers
b. November 2, 1942

Actress best known for her role in the
mystery series Hart to Hart.

Bob Gaudio
b. November 17, 1942

Singer, songwriter, musician and record
producer (The Four Seasons).

Martin Scorsese
b. November 17, 1942

Film director, producer, screenwriter and
actor.

Linda Evans
b. November 18, 1942

Actress best known for portraying Krystle Carrington in the soap opera Dynasty.

Susan Sullivan
b. November 18, 1942

Actress.

Calvin Klein
b. November 19, 1942

Fashion designer.

Joe Biden
b. November 20, 1942

Politician serving as the 46th President of the United States.

Jimi Hendrix
b. November 27, 1942
d. September 18, 1970
Musician, singer and songwriter.

Michael Nesmith
b. December 30, 1942

Musician, songwriter, actor, producer, novelist, businessman and philanthropist.

Notable American Deaths

Jan 4	Melvin Whinfield "Peerless Mel" Sheppard (b. September 5, 1883) - Athlete who won three gold medals at the 1908 Summer Olympics, and one gold and one silver medal at the 1912 Summer Olympics. *NB: Along with Henry Taylor of the United Kingdom he was the most successful athlete at the 1908 games.*
Jan 4	Otis Skinner (b. June 28, 1858) - Stage actor active during the late nineteenth and early twentieth centuries.
Jan 6	John Bernard Flannagan (b. April 7, 1895) - Sculptor who is known as one of the first practitioners of direct carving (taille directe) in the United States.
Jan 8	Joseph Franklin Rutherford (b. November 8, 1869) - The second president of the incorporated Watch Tower Bible and Tract Society of Pennsylvania. Rutherford played a primary role in the organization and doctrinal development of Jehovah's Witnesses.

January 16: Carole Lombard (b. Jane Alice Peters; October 6, 1908) - Actress particularly noted for her energetic, often off-beat roles, in screwball comedies. Lombard was among the most commercially successful and admired film personalities in Hollywood in the 1930s.

In 1999, the American Film Institute ranked Lombard 23rd on its list of the 25 greatest American female screen legends of classic Hollywood cinema.

Jan 29	Bion Joseph Arnold (b. August 14, 1861) - Engineer remembered as the "father of the third rail", a pioneer in electrical engineering, and an urban mass transportation expert who helped design New York's Interborough Rapid Transit subway system.
Jan 29	Mason Mathews Patrick (b. December 13, 1863) - General officer in the Army who led the Army Air Service during and after World War I, and became the first Chief of the Army Air Corps when it was created on July 2, 1926.
Feb 9	Anna Elizabeth Klumpke (b. October 28, 1856) - Portrait and genre painter, perhaps best known for her portraits of famous women including Elizabeth Cady Stanton (1889) and Rosa Bonheur (1898).
Feb 10	Lawrence Joseph Henderson (b. June 3, 1878) - Physiologist, chemist, biologist, philosopher and sociologist who was one of the leading biochemists of the early 20th century.
Feb 12	Grant DeVolson Wood (b. February 13, 1891) - Painter best known for his works depicting the rural Midwest, particularly American Gothic (1930) which has become an iconic example of 20th century American art.
Feb 18	Albert Payson Terhune (b. December 21, 1872) - Author, dog breeder and journalist.
Feb 19	Frank Abbandando (b. July 11, 1910) - New York City contract killer nicknamed "The Dasher" who committed many murders as part of the infamous Murder, Inc. organized crime group.

Feb 27	Martha McChesney Berry (b. October 7, 1865) - Educator and the founder of Berry College in Rome, Georgia.
Mar 1	George Snavely Rentz (b. July 25, 1882) - Navy chaplain who served during World War I and World War II. For selfless heroism following the loss of USS Houston (CA-30) in the Battle of Sunda Strait, he was posthumously awarded the Navy Cross - the only Navy Chaplain to be so honored during WWII.
Mar 2	Charles Henry Christian (b. July 29, 1916) - Swing and jazz guitarist who was inducted into the Rock and Roll Hall of Fame in 1990 in the category Early Influence.
Mar 6	Thomas Joseph "Tom" Mooney (b. December 8, 1882) - Political activist and labor leader who was convicted with Warren K. Billings of the San Francisco Preparedness Day Bombing of 1916. Believed by many to have been wrongly convicted of a crime he did not commit, Mooney served 22 years in prison before finally being pardoned in 1939.
Mar 7	Lucy Eldine Gonzalez Parsons (b. Lucia Carter; 1851) - Labor organizer, radical socialist and anarcho-communist.
Mar 19	Clinton Hart Merriam (b. December 5, 1855) - Zoologist, mammalogist, ornithologist, entomologist, ecologist, ethnographer, geographer and naturalist.
Mar 26	Carolyn Wells (b. June 18, 1862) - Prolific novelist and poet.
Apr 6	Rear Admiral Bradley Allen Fiske (b. June 13, 1854) - Navy officer who was noted as a technical innovator. During his career Fiske invented more than 130 electrical and mechanical devices serving both naval and civilian uses.
Apr 15	Hugh Samuel Johnson (b. August 5, 1882) - Army officer, businessman, speech writer, government official and newspaper columnist best known as a member of the Brain Trust of Franklin D. Roosevelt (1932-1934).
Apr 18	Gertrude Vanderbilt Whitney (b. January 9, 1875) - Sculptor, art patron, collector and founder of the Whitney Museum of American Art in New York City in 1931.
Apr 21	Gustav Stickley (b. March 9, 1858) - Furniture manufacturer, design leader, publisher and a leading voice in the American Arts and Crafts movement.
Apr 27	Arthur LeRoy Bristol, Jr. (b. July 15, 1886) - Navy Vice Admiral who held important commands during World War I and World War II, and was an early aircraft carrier commander.
May 9	Graham McNamee (b. July 10, 1888) - Radio broadcaster and personality who originated play-by-play sports broadcasting. McNamee was inducted into The National Radio Hall of Fame in 2011.
May 29	John Barrymore (b. John Sidney Blyth; February 15, 1882) - Actor on stage, screen and radio.
Jun 4	Edgar R. Bassett (b. March 10, 1914) - Navy officer who received the Navy Cross posthumously for "extraordinary heroism and devotion to duty" during the Battle of the Coral Sea.
Jun 4	Virginia Lee Corbin (b. December 5, 1910) - Silent film actress.
Jun 18	Arthur Willard Pryor (b. September 22, 1869) - Trombone virtuoso, bandleader and soloist with the Sousa Band. He was a prolific composer of band music, his best-known composition being "The Whistler and His Dog".
Jun 19	Francis "Frank" Cleveland Irons (b. March 23, 1886) - Athlete who won a gold medal in the long jump at the 1908 Summer Olympics in London, England.
Jun 23	William L Couper (b. September 20, 1853) - Sculptor.
Jun 30	William Henry Jackson (b. April 4, 1843) - Painter, Civil War veteran, geological survey photographer and an explorer famous for his images of the American West.

Jul 18	George Alexander Sutherland (b. March 25, 1862) - English-born jurist and politician who served as an Associate Justice of the United States Supreme Court (1922-1938).
Jul 30	James Blanton (b. October 5, 1918) - Jazz double bassist.
Aug 22	Henry Eichheim (b. January 3, 1870) - Composer, conductor, violinist, organologist, and ethnomusicologist best known as one of the first American composers to combine the sound of indigenous Asian instruments with western orchestral colors.
Aug 22	Alice Duer Miller (b. July 28, 1874) - Writer whose feminist verses made an impact on the suffrage issue, and her verse novel The White Cliffs encouraged the United States' entry into World War II.
Sep 14	Ezra Seymour Gosney (b. November 6, 1855) - Philanthropist and eugenicist.
Sep 17	Cecilia Beaux (b. May 1, 1855) - Society portraitist whose subjects included First Lady Edith Roosevelt, Admiral Sir David Beatty, and Georges Clemenceau.
Sep 19	Condé Montrose Nast (b. March 26, 1873) - Publisher, entrepreneur and business magnate who founded Condé Nast; Vanity Fair, Vogue, The New Yorker…
Sep 27	Douglas Albert Munro (b. October 11, 1919) - Coast Guardsman who was posthumously decorated with the Medal of Honor (the only person to have received the medal for actions performed during service in the Coast Guard).
Sep 28	Eva Thatcher (b. March 14, 1862) - Film actress and vaudeville performer who appeared in more than 100 films (1912-1930).
Oct 5	Dorothea Klumpke Roberts (b. August 9, 1861) - Astronomer who was made a Chevalier de la Légion d'Honneur, and was the Director of the Bureau of Measurements at the Paris Observatory.
Oct 23	Ralph Rainger (b. Reichenthal; October 7, 1901) - Composer of popular music, principally for films.

November 5: George Michael Cohan (b. July 3, 1878) - Entertainer, playwright, composer, lyricist, actor, singer, dancer and theatrical producer who is considered the father of American musical comedy.

Cohan's life and music were depicted in the Oscar-winning film Yankee Doodle Dandy (1942) and the 1968 musical George M!. A statue of Cohan in Times Square, New York City, commemorates his contributions to American musical theatre.

Nov 9	Edna May Oliver (b. Edna May Nutter; November 9, 1883) - Stage and film actress.
Nov 12	Joseph Francis Hagan (b. January 17, 1878) - World light heavyweight boxing champion better known as Philadelphia Jack O'Brien. O'Brien was inducted into the Ring Magazine Hall of Fame in 1968, the World Boxing Hall of Fame in 1987, and the International Boxing Hall of Fame in 1994.
Nov 13	Daniel Judson Callaghan (b. July 26, 1890) - Navy Rear Admiral who received the Medal of Honor posthumously for his actions during the Naval Battle of Guadalcanal.
Nov 13	Norman (Nicholas) Scott (b. August 10, 1889) - Navy Rear Admiral who received the Medal of Honor posthumously for his actions during the Naval Battle of Guadalcanal.

Nov 30	Buck Jones (b. Charles Frederick Gebhart; December 12, 1891) - Actor, known for his work in many popular Western movies (in his early film appearances he was credited as Charles Jones). *NB: Jones was one of the 492 victims of the Cocoanut Grove fire in Boston, Massachusetts on November 28, 1942.*
Dec 5	Richard Tucker (b. June 4, 1884) - Actor who appeared in 266 films (1911-1940) and was the first official member of the Screen Actors Guild (SAG) and a founding member of SAG's Board of Directors.
Dec 6	Amos Wilson Rusie (b. May 30, 1871) - Right-handed pitcher nicknamed "The Hoosier Thunderbolt" who played in Major League Baseball during the late 19th century. For his accomplishments he was inducted into the Baseball Hall of Fame in 1977 by the Veterans Committee.
Dec 8	Albert Kahn (b. March 21, 1869) - The foremost American industrial architect of his day, sometimes referred to as the "architect of Detroit."
Dec 12	Helen Westley (b. Henrietta Remsen Meserole Manney; March 28, 1875) - Character actress who was a founding member of the original board of the Theatre Guild.
Dec 13	Robert Robinson Taylor (b. June 8, 1868) - Architect and educator who was the first African-American student enrolled at the Massachusetts Institute of Technology, and the first accredited African-American architect when he graduated in 1892.
Dec 20	Dan Ahearn (b. Daniel William Ahearne; April 12, 1888) - Track and field athlete who was a member of the Irish American Athletic Club. He competed at the 1920 Summer Olympics in Antwerp, Belgium, and was the men's triple jump world record holder (1909-1924).
Dec 21	Franz Uri Boas (b. July 9, 1858) - German-born American pioneer of modern anthropology who has been called the "Father of American Anthropology."
Dec 27	William George Morgan (b. January 23, 1870) - The inventor of volleyball (originally called Mintonette) who was inducted into the Volleyball Hall of Fame in 1985 as its inaugural member.

POPULAR MUSIC

Bing Crosby	No.1	White Christmas
Glenn Miller	No.2	(I've Got A Gal In) Kalamazoo
Jimmy Dorsey	No.3	Tangerine
Glenn Miller	No.4	Moonlight Cocktail
Harry James	No.5	Sleepy Lagoon
Kay Kyser	No.6	Jingle Jangle Jingle
Benny Goodman	No.7	Jersey Bounce
Woody Herman	No.8	Blues In The Night
Alvino Rey	No.9	Deep In The Heart Of Texas
Bing Crosby	No.10	Moonlight Becomes You

N.B. During this era music was dominated by a number of Big Bands and songs could be attributed to the band leader, the band name, the lead singer or a combination of these. On top of this the success of a song was tied to the sales of sheet music, so a popular song would often be perfomed by many different combinations of singers and bands, and the contemporary charts would list the song without clarifying whose version was the major hit. With this in mind although the above chart has been compiled with best intent it does remain subjective.

Bing Crosby
White Christmas

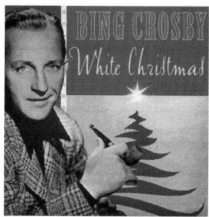 

Label:	Written by:	Length:
Decca	Irving Berlin	3 mins 3 secs

Harry Lillis "Bing" Crosby, Jr. (b. May 3, 1903 - d. October 14, 1977) was a singer, comedian and an Oscar winning actor who also bred racehorses and co-owned the Pittsburgh Pirates baseball team. His trademark warm bass-baritone voice made him the best-selling recording artist of the 20th century; Crosby has sold over one billion records, tapes, compact discs and digital downloads around the world.

Glenn Miller
(I've Got A Gal In) Kalamazoo

Label:	Written by:	Length:
Victor	Warren / Gordon	3 mins 13 secs

Alton Glenn Miller (b. March 1, 1904 - MIA December 15, 1944) was a big-band musician, arranger, composer and bandleader. He was the best-selling recording artist from 1939 to 1943, leading one of the most popular and commercially successful dance orchestras of the swing era; in the space of just four years Miller scored 16 number-one records and 69 top ten hits.

Jimmy Dorsey
Tangerine

Label:	Written by:	Length:
Decca	Mercer / Schertzinger	3 mins 7 secs

James Francis Dorsey (b. February 29, 1904 - d. June 12, 1957) was a jazz clarinetist, saxophonist, composer and big band leader known professionally as Jimmy Dorsey. He was inducted into the Big Band Hall of Fame in 1983 and is considered one of the most important and influential alto saxophone players of the Big Band and Swing era. Dorsey notably played clarinet on the seminal jazz standards Singin' the Blues (1927) and the original recording of Georgia on My Mind (1930), both of which were inducted into the Grammy Hall of Fame.

Glenn Miller
Moonlight Cocktail

Label:	Written by:	Length:
Bluebird	Roberts / Gannon	3 mins 14 secs

In 1942, **Glenn Miller** volunteered to join the military to entertain troops during World War II, ending up in the U.S. Army Air Forces. On December 15, 1944, while flying to Paris, Miller's aircraft disappeared in bad weather over the English Channel. He was posthumously awarded the Bronze Star Medal.

Harry James
Sleepy Lagoon

Label:	Written by:	Length:
Columbia	Lawrence / Coates	2 mins 55 secs

Harry Haag James (b. March 15, 1916 - d. July 5, 1983) was a musician who is best known as a trumpet-playing band leader who led a big band from 1939 to 1946. He broke up his band for a short period in 1947 but shortly after he reorganized and was active again from then until his death in 1983. James was especially known among musicians for his technical proficiency as well as his tone, and he was influential on new trumpet players from the late 1930s into the 1940s.

Kay Kyser
Jingle Jangle Jingle

Label:	Written by:	Length:
Columbia	Loesser / Lilley	3 mins 14 secs

James Kern "Kay" Kyser (b. June 18, 1905 - d. July 23, 1985) was a bandleader and radio personality of the 1930s and 1940s. With his Orchestra he had 11 number-one records, including some of the most popular songs of the late 1930s and early 1940s. Kyser also appeared in several motion pictures with his band, usually as themselves. The song Jingle Jangle Jingle appeared in the 1942 movie The Forest Rangers. Although it was recorded by many musicians, Kyser's version was the most commercially successful.

7   Benny Goodman
Jersey Bounce

Label:	Written by:	Length:
Okeh	Plater / Johnson / Wright / Bradshaw	2 mins 52 secs

Benjamin David "Benny" Goodman (b. May 30, 1909 - d. June 13, 1986) was a jazz and swing musician, clarinetist and bandleader known as the King of Swing. His bands launched the careers of many major names in jazz and, during an era of segregation, he also led one of the first well-known integrated jazz groups. Goodman's instrumental Jersey Bounce spent a total of 20 weeks in the Billboard charts from the Spring of 1942.

8   Woody Herman
Blues In The Night

Label:	Written by:	Length:
Decca	Arlen / Mercer	3 mins 15 secs

Woodrow Charles Herman (b. May 16, 1913 - d. October 29, 1987) was a jazz clarinetist, saxophonist, singer and big band leader. Leading various groups called "The Herd", Herman came to prominence in the late 1930s and was active until his death in 1987. His bands received numerous Grammy nominations and awards, and often played music that was cutting edge and experimental for its time.

Alvino Rey
Deep In The Heart Of Texas

Label:	Written by:	Length:
Bluebird	Swander / Hershey	2 mins 34 secs

Alvin McBurney (b. July 1, 1908 - d. February 24, 2004) was a jazz guitarist and bandleader known by his stage name Alvino Rey. Rey was pioneer of electrified instruments having first amplified his banjo in the 1920s. In 1935, Gibson hired him to develop a prototype pickup based on the one he developed for his banjo. The result was used for Gibson's first electric guitar, the ES-150.

Bing Crosby
Moonlight Becomes You

Label:	Written by:	Length:
Decca	Van Heusen / Burke	3 mins 9 secs

Bing Crosby was the first real multimedia star and a leader in record sales, radio ratings, and motion picture grosses from 1931 to 1954. His early career coincided with recording innovations that allowed him to develop an intimate singing style that influenced many male singers who followed him including Perry Como, Frank Sinatra, Dick Haymes, and Dean Martin. For his achievements Crosby has been recognized with three stars on the Hollywood Walk of Fame; for motion pictures, radio, and audio recording.

1942: TOP FILMS

1. **Mrs. Miniver** - *Metro-Goldwyn-Mayer*
2. **Yankee Doodle Dandy** - *Warner Bros.*
3. **Random Harvest** - *Metro-Goldwyn-Mayer*
4. **Reap the Wild Wind** - *Paramount Pictures*
5. **Holiday Inn** - *Paramount Pictures*

OSCARS

Best Picture: Mrs. Miniver
Most Nominations: Mrs. Miniver (12)
Most Wins: Mrs. Miniver (6)

Oscar winners (from left): Heflin, Garson, Cagney and Wright.

Best Director: William Wyler - *Mrs. Miniver*

Best Actor: James Cagney - *Yankee Doodle Dandy*
Best Actress: Greer Garson - *Mrs. Miniver*
Best Supporting Actor: Van Heflin - *Johnny Eager*
Best Supporting Actress: Teresa Wright - *Mrs. Miniver*

The 15th Academy Awards, honoring the best in film for 1942, were presented March 4, 1943 at The Ambassador Hotel in Los Angeles, California.

Directed by: William Wyler - Runtime: 2h 14m

The Minivers, an English middle-class family, experience life in the first months of World War II.

Starring

Greer Garson
b. September 29, 1904
d. April 6, 1966
Character:
Mrs. Miniver

Walter Pidgeon
b. September 23, 1897
d. September 25, 1984
Character:
Clem Miniver

Teresa Wright
b. October 27, 1918
d. March 6, 2005
Character:
Carol Beldon

Trivia

Goof | In the radio broadcast by Lord Haw Haw he mentions the fall of France. A day or so later the boats are called out to help in the evacuation of Dunkirk (Operation Dynamo). France did not fall until two weeks after Dunkirk.

Interesting Facts | After first-choice Norma Shearer rejected the title role of Mrs. Miniver because she refused to play a mother, Greer Garson was cast. Although Garson didn't want the part either she was contractually bound to take it and won her only Oscar for her performance. *NB: Garson was nominated a total of 7 times for the Academy Award for Best Actress throughout her career.*

Winston Churchill once said that this film had done more for the war effort than a flotilla of destroyers.

After completing the film, William Wyler joined the U.S. Army and was overseas on the night he won his first Oscar. He later revealed that his subsequent war experiences made him realize that the film actually portrayed war in too soft a light. *NB: Wyler went on to win two more Academy Awards for Best Director; The Best Years of Our Lives (1946), Ben-Hur (1959).*

Shortly after shooting was completed, Greer Garson married Richard Ney, who plays her son, Vin, in the film.

Mrs. Miniver is first of only two Academy Award Best Picture winners to receive nominations in all four acting categories. The other is From Here to Eternity (1953).

Quote | **Carol Beldon**: I know how comfortable it is to curl up with a nice, fat book full of big words and think you're going to solve all the problems in the universe. But you're not, you know. A bit of action is required every now and then.

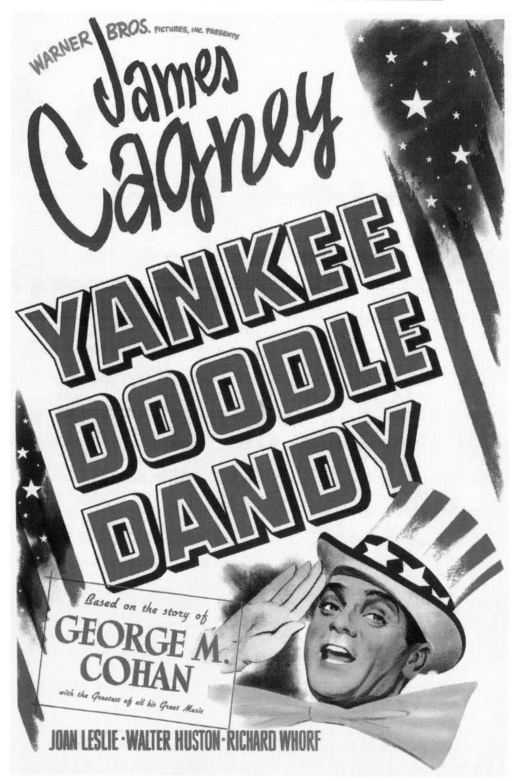

Directed by: Michael Curtiz - Runtime: 2h 6m

The life of the renowned musical composer, playwright, actor, dancer and singer, George M. Cohan.

Starring

James Cagney
b. July 17, 1899
d. March 30, 1986
Character:
George M. Cohan

Joan Leslie
b. January 26, 1925
d. October 12, 2015
Character:
Mary Cohan

Walter Huston
b. April 5, 1883
d. April 7, 1950
Character:
Jerry Cohan

Trivia

Goof | In the "You're A Grand Old Flag" number, which supposedly takes place in the 1906 production of George Washington Jr., we see a group of Boy Scouts march onto the stage. The Scout Movement was founded in 1907 by Robert Baden-Powell in England and wasn't founded in the United States until 1910.

Interesting Facts | Despite failing health, the real George M. Cohan acted briefly as a consultant on the film. He lived long enough to see the finished result and approved wholeheartedly of James Cagney's depiction of himself.

Joan Leslie portrays Mary Cohan, aging from 18 to 57 throughout proceedings. Leslie turned 17 during the production of the movie. The fact that she was still attending school during filming caused numerous delays.

Future director Don Siegel was responsible for putting together the numerous montages that appear throughout the film.

James Cagney became the first actor to win the Best Actor Academy Award for a musical performance.

According to his biography the rather stiff-legged dancing style used by James Cagney in this movie is not his own. He copied George M. Cohan's style to make the film more accurate.

Quotes | *[first lines]*
Critic #1: I call it a hit. What'll your review say?
Critic #2: I like it too, so I guess I'll pan it. it.

George M. Cohan: My mother thanks you, my father thanks you, my sister thanks you, and I thank you.

Random Harvest

Another triumph from Metro-Goldwyn-Mayer
—the producers of "Mrs. Miniver"

RONALD COLMAN
GREER GARSON

IN JAMES HILTON'S

RANDOM HARVEST

Directed by MERVYN LeROY
Produced by SIDNEY FRANKLIN
PHILIP DORN
SUSAN PETERS
HENRY TRAVERS
REGINALD OWEN
BRAMWELL FLETCHER

A MERVYN LeRoy PRODUCTION

A Metro-Goldwyn-Mayer PICTURE

Directed by: Mervyn LeRoy - Runtime: 2h 6m

An amnesiac World War I veteran falls in love with a music hall star, only to suffer an accident which restores his original memories but erases his post-war life.

Starring

Ronald Colman
b. February 9, 1891
d. May 19, 1958
Character:
Charles Rainier /
"John Smith" (Smithy)

Greer Garson
b. September 29, 1904
d. April 6, 1966
Character:
"Paula Ridgeway" /
Margaret Hanson

Philip Dorn
b. September 30, 1901
d. May 9, 1975
Character:
Dr. Jonathan Benet

Trivia

Goof | In the last scene where Smithy goes back to the cottage, the flowering tree on the path has not changed or grown at all in the 15 years since he was last there.

Interesting Facts | The person Greer Garson spent the most time with on set was cameraman Joseph Ruttenberg who was her favorite photographer. She appreciated his using a woman's stocking over the lens to soften and glamorize her features. In addition, he quickly realized that she looked best shot from the right and made sure the sets were constructed so he could favor that side.

Like most Hollywood movies of the era, it was shot entirely on a studio backlot, where designers and technicians created their own versions of the streets of Liverpool, London's Waterloo Station and the cottage where Paula and Smithy found happiness.

When the writers had trouble coming up with a scene to show Paula on stage, Greer Garson suggested singing the Harry Lauder standard "She M' Daisy" in a short kilt. Sidney Franklin and Louis B. Mayer hesitated, concerned that the show of leg would hurt her image as the perfect lady. They even tried kilts in three different lengths, finally choosing a medium-length one that wouldn't show too much leg.

Ronald Colman had first-hand experience of shell shock - he had fought in the British army at the Battle of Ypres in World War I, during which he was also gassed.

Quote | **Smithy**: I don't even know who I am.
Paula: Well, I know who you are. You're someone awfully nice.

Directed by: Cecil B. DeMille - Runtime: 2h 3m

Florida ship salvager Loxi Claiborne falls for Jack Stuart, the captain of a ship wrecked on the Key West shore. However, their romance is complicated by the arrival of another suitor, and eventually leads to tragedy.

Starring

Ray Milland
b. January 3, 1907
d. March 10, 1986
Character:
Stephen Tolliver

John Wayne
b. May 26, 1907
d. June 11, 1979
Character:
Jack Stuart

Paulette Goddard
b. June 3, 1910
d. April 23, 1990
Character:
Loxi Claiborne

Trivia

Goofs

The first time Loxi talks to Jack, her hat ribbon repeatedly changes position around her neck between shots. The second time Loxi talks to Jack, she points at him with the index finger of her left hand. In the next shot it is her right hand.

Interesting Facts

John Wayne did not like Cecil B. DeMille. He felt the director had passed him over for the role of Wild Bill Hickok in The Plainsman (1936), which Wayne had felt certain would have made him a star.

Cecil B. DeMille had wanted Errol Flynn to play Captain Jack Stuart, but Jack L. Warner refused to loan him out.

The shots of the giant squid wrapping its tentacles around the actors was done by wrapping the actors in the tentacles, then unwrapping them and showing the film in reverse. *NB: The rubber squid was donated by the studio to the war effort in 1942 because the Japanese had conquered Malaya and Indochina, the source of most of the world's rubber.*

Although John Wayne was pleased to have been cast in such an important movie, he was unhappy with his part and once complained he was only there to make Ray Milland look like a "real man".

During the filming of a fight scene with John Wayne, an accident cost actor Victor Kilian (Widgeon) the use of one eye.

For the 1954 theatrical re-release, John Wayne was given top billing in the posters because of his increased star status, and Susan Hayward, who had become a major star instead of a supporting player, was misleadingly billed second. Formerly top-billed Ray Milland got third billing in the new posters, whilst leading lady Paulette Goddard was demoted to fourth billing.

Directed by: Mark Sandrich - Runtime: 1h 40m

At an inn which is open only on holidays, a crooner and a dancer vie for the affections of a beautiful up-and-coming performer.

Starring

Bing Crosby
b. May 3, 1903
d. October 14, 1977
Character:
Jim Hardy

Fred Astaire
b. May 10, 1899
d. June 22, 1987
Character:
Ted Hanover

Marjorie Reynolds
b. August 12, 1917
d. February 1, 1997
Character:
Linda Mason

Trivia

Goof | When Jim first plays "White Christmas" with Linda at the inn, he sits down to play a piano. However, there is no piano present on the audio track.

Interesting Facts | Director Mark Sandrich originally wanted Ginger Rogers and Rita Hayworth as the female leads. However, executives at Paramount vetoed this idea, since Bing Crosby and Fred Astaire, two of the studio's highest-paid stars, were already co-starring in the movie.

For the "drunk" dance, Fred Astaire had two drinks of bourbon before the first take and one before each succeeding take. The seventh and last take was eventually used in the film.

Both of the leading ladies have their hair dyed opposite to their natural hair colour: Marjorie Reynolds is a brunette playing the blonde Linda Mason; Virginia Dale is a blonde playing brunette Lila Dixon.

When Irving Berlin won an Oscar for his song "White Christmas" he became the first ever artist to present himself with an Academy Award.

The Connecticut Inn set for this movie was reused by Paramount 12 years later as a Vermont Inn for the musical White Christmas (1954), also starring Bing Crosby and again with songs composed by Irving Berlin.

The Holiday Inn motel chain (established in 1952) was named after this movie.

Quote | **Linda Mason**: What would you like?
Danny Reed: Orchids, the finest you've got.
Linda Mason: Corsage?
Danny Reed: No, no. A dozen, loose, looking like they don't care!

SPORTING WINNERS

AP Associated Press

MALE ATHLETE OF THE YEAR

Frank Sinkwich - College Football

Frank Francis Sinkwich Sr. (b. October 10, 1920 - d. October 22, 1990) was a football player and coach. He won the Heisman Trophy in 1942 playing for the University of Georgia, making him the first recipient from the Southeastern Conference. After his collegiate career Sinkwich joined the Marine Corps, however, due to his flat feet he received a medical discharge and proceeded to play with the Detroit Lions (who had selected him first overall in the 1943 NFL Draft). In Detroit he earned All-Pro honors in 1943-1944, as well as being named as NFL MVP in 1944. Sinkwich was inducted into the College Football Hall of Fame in 1954.

Career Highlights / Awards:

NFL Most Valuable Player	1944
First-team All-Pro	1943, 1944
National champion	1942
Heisman Trophy	1942
Sporting News Player of the Year	1942
Associated Press Athlete of the Year	1942
Consensus All-American	1941, 1942
Georgia Bulldogs No.21	Retired

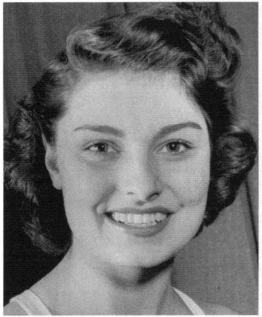

Gloria Callen - Swimming

Gloria Callen (b. December 21, 1923 - d. September 2, 2016) was a backstroke swimmer who was voted the 1942 Associated Press Female Athlete of the Year. She set 35 American records and one world record in swimming, and won 13 American championships. Due to World War II, she was never able to compete in world championships or Olympic Games, even though she qualified for the 1940 Olympic Games. Callen's swimming career ended when she enrolled at Barnard College and joined the American Women's Voluntary Services (AWVS).

"Glorious Gloria" Callen was one in a row of glamorous swimming champions; aged 19 she won the New York Fashion Academy Award as one of America's 13 best dressed women. Callen was inducted into International Swimming Hall of Fame in 1984.

BOSTON MARATHON

1st	Bernard Smith	Massachusetts	2h 26m 51s
2nd	Louis Gregory	New York	2h 28m 3s
3rd	Carl Maroney	Massachusetts	2h 36m 13s

The Boston Marathon is the oldest annual marathon in the world and dates back to 1897.

GOLF

The Masters - Byron Nelson

The Masters Tournament is the first of the majors to be played each year and unlike the other major championships it is played at the same location - Augusta National Golf Club, Georgia. This was the 9th Masters Tournament and it was held April 9-13, 1942. Byron Nelson, the 1937 champion, won an 18-hole playoff by one stroke over runner-up Ben Hogan to take home the $1,500 winner's share of the $5,000 purse.

PGA Championship - Sam Snead

The 1942 and 25th PGA Championship was played May 25-31 at Seaview Country Club in Galloway Township, New Jersey, just north of Atlantic City. Then a match play championship, Sam Snead won the first of his seven major titles, 2 & 1, in the final over Jim Turnesa. The winner's share of the $7,550 prize fund was $2,000.

U.S. Open - Canceled

The 1942 U.S. Open Championship (established in 1895) was cancelled due to World War II.

Sam Snead

Byron Nelson

MLB - WORLD SERIES

St. Louis Cardinals   4 - 1   New York Yankees

Total attendance: 277,101 - Average attendance: 55,420
Winning player's share: $6,193 - Losing player's share: $3,352

The 1942 World Series matched the National League champions, the St. Louis Cardinals, against the American League champions, the New York Yankees. The Cardinals won in five games for their first championship since 1934 and their fourth overall.

	Date	Score			Location	Time	Att.
1	Sep 30	**Yankees**	7-4	Cardinals	Sportsman's Park	2:35	34,769
2	Oct 1	Yankees	3-4	**Cardinals**	Sportsman's Park	1:57	34,255
3	Oct 3	**Cardinals**	2-0	Yankees	Yankee Stadium	2:30	69,123
4	Oct 4	**Cardinals**	9-6	Yankees	Yankee Stadium	2:28	69,902
5	Oct 5	**Cardinals**	4-2	Yankees	Yankee Stadium	1:58	69,052

Season Summary

Pos.	American League	W	L	PCT	GB
1st	**New York Yankees**	103	51	.669	-
2nd	Boston Red Sox	93	59	.612	9
3rd	St. Louis Browns	82	69	.543	19½
4th	Cleveland Indians	75	79	.487	28

MVP: Joe Gordon, New York Yankees

Pos.	National League	W	L	PCT	GB
1st	**St. Louis Cardinals**	106	48	.688	-
2nd	Brooklyn Dodgers	104	50	.675	2
3rd	New York Giants	85	67	.559	20
4th	Cincinnati Reds	76	76	.500	29

MVP: Mort Cooper, St. Louis Cardinals

Horse Racing

Shut Out (b. February 27, 1939 - d. April 23, 1964) was an American Thoroughbred racehorse and sire who came close to winning the 1942 Triple Crown (losing out in just the Preakness Stakes to Alsab, when he finished fifth after a troubled trip).

Alsab (b. 1939 - d. 1963) was an American Thoroughbred racehorse who was voted the 1942 U.S. Champion Three-Year-Old Colt. Alsab was inducted in the United States' National Museum of Racing and Hall of Fame in 1976.

Kentucky Derby: Shut Out

The Kentucky Derby is held annually at Churchill Downs in Louisville, Kentucky, on the first Saturday in May. The race is a Grade 1 stakes race for three-year-olds and is one and a quarter mile in length.

Preakness Stakes - Alsab

The Preakness Stakes is held on the third Saturday in May each year at Pimlico Race Course in Baltimore, Maryland. It is a Grade 1 race run over a distance of 9.5 furlongs (1 3/16 mile) on dirt.

Belmont Stakes - Shut Out

The Belmont Stakes is Grade 1 race held every June at Belmont Park in Elmont, New York. It is 1.5 mile in length and is open to three-year-old thoroughbreds. It takes place on a Saturday between June 5 and June 11.

Indianapolis 500

The 1942 Indianapolis 500 was scheduled for Saturday May 30, 1942, at the Indianapolis Motor Speedway. It was to be the 30th annual running of the famous automobile race but the race was canceled due to the United States involvement in World War II; the race would not be held again until 1946.

This was the second instance in which the Indianapolis Motor Speedway suspended the annual running of the Indianapolis 500. During World War I the Speedway management voluntarily suspended competition in 1917 and 1918. However, for World War II, the decision to cancel the race was more resolute, and ultimately was part of a four-year nationwide ban on automobile racing.

NFL - CHAMPIONSHIP GAME

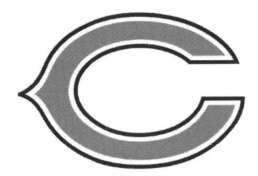

Chicago Bears   6 - 14   **Washington Redskins**

Played: December 13, 1942 at at Griffith Stadium in Washington, D.C.
Winning player's share: $976 - Losing player's share: $639
Attendance: 36,006 / Referee: Ronald Gibbs

Season Summary

The 1942 NFL season was the 23rd regular season of the National Football League and was played September 13 through December 13, 1942. The season concluded with the NFL Championship Game which saw the Washington Redskins defeat the Chicago Bears 14-6.

Eastern Division

Team	P	W	L	T	PCT	PF	PA
Washington Redskins	11	10	1	0	.909	227	102
Pittsburgh Steelers	11	7	4	0	.636	167	119
New York Giants	11	5	5	1	.500	155	139

Western Division

Team	P	W	L	T	PCT	PF	PA
Chicago Bears	11	11	0	0	1.000	376	84
Green Bay Packers	11	8	2	1	.800	300	215
Cleveland Rams	11	5	6	0	.455	150	207

Joe F. Carr Trophy (Most Valuable Player): Don Hutson - Green Bay Packers
Note: The NFL did not officially count tie games in the standings until 1972.

League Leaders

Statistic	Name	Team	Yards
Passing	Cecil Isbell	Green Bay Packers	2021
Rushing	Bill Dudley	Pittsburgh Steelers	696
Receiving	Don Hutson	Green Bay Packers	1211

NHL - STANLEY CUP

Toronto Maple Leafs **4 - 3** **Detroit Red Wings**

	Date	Team	Result	Team	Stadium
1	Apr 4	**Detroit Red Wings**	3-2	Toronto Maple Leafs	Maple Leaf Gardens
2	Apr 7	**Detroit Red Wings**	4-2	Toronto Maple Leafs	Maple Leaf Gardens
3	Apr 9	Toronto Maple Leafs	2-5	**Detroit Red Wings**	Olympia Stadium
4	Apr 12	**Toronto Maple Leafs**	4-3	Detroit Red Wings	Olympia Stadium
5	Apr 14	Detroit Red Wings	3-9	**Toronto Maple Leafs**	Maple Leaf Gardens
6	Apr 16	**Toronto Maple Leafs**	3-0	Detroit Red Wings	Olympia Stadium
7	Apr 18	Detroit Red Wings	1-3	**Toronto Maple Leafs**	Maple Leaf Gardens

Season Summary

The 1941-1942 NHL season was the 25th season of the National Hockey League and featured 7 teams each playing 48 games. The Toronto Maple Leafs won the Stanley Cup, winning four straight games after losing the first three in the best-of-seven series.

Final Standings:

	Team	GP	W	L	T	GF	GA	Pts
1	**New York Rangers**	48	29	17	2	177	143	60
2	Toronto Maple Leafs	48	27	18	3	158	136	57
3	Boston Bruins	48	25	17	6	160	118	56
4	Chicago Black Hawks	48	22	23	3	145	155	47

Scoring Leaders:

	Player	Team	GP	Goals	Assists	Pts	PIM
1	**Bryan Hextall**	**New York Rangers**	48	24	32	56	30
2	Lynn Patrick	New York Rangers	47	32	22	54	18
3	Don Grosso	Detroit Red Wings	45	23	30	53	13

Hart Trophy (Most Valuable Player): Tommy Anderson, Brooklyn Americans
Vezina Trophy (Fewest Goals Allowed): Frank Brimsek, Boston Bruins

TENNIS - NATIONAL CHAMPIONSHIPS

Pauline Betz *(U.S. National Championships 1943)* / Ted Schroeder *(Wimbledon 1949).*

The 1942 U.S. National Championships (now known as the US Open) took place on the outdoor grass courts at the West Side Tennis Club, Forest Hills in New York. The tournament ran from August 27 through September 7, and was the 62nd staging of the Championships. *NB: Due to the war it was the only Grand Slam tennis event of the year.*

Men's Singles Final

Country	Player	Set 1	Set 2	Set 3	Set 4	Set 5
United States	Ted Schroeder	8	7	3	4	6
United States	Frank Parker	6	5	6	6	2

Women's Singles Final

Country	Player	Set 1	Set 2	Set 3
United States	Pauline Betz	4	6	6
United States	Louise Brough	6	1	4

Men's Doubles Final

Country	Players	Set 1	Set 2	Set 3
United States	Gardnar Mulloy / Bill Talbert	9	7	6
United States	Ted Schroeder / Sidney Wood	7	5	1

Women's Doubles Final

Country	Players	Set 1	Set 2	Set 3
United States	Louise Brough / Margaret Osborne	2	7	6
United States	Pauline Betz / Doris Hart	6	5	0

Mixed Doubles Final

Country	Players	Set 1	Set 2	Set 3
United States	Louise Brough / Ted Schroeder	3	6	6
United States / Argentina	Patricia Todd / Alejo Russell	6	1	4

THE COST OF LIVING

Comparison Chart

	1942	1942 + Inflation	2021	% Change
House	$9,350	$150,049	$295,300	+96.8%
Annual Income	$1,200	$19,258	$64,740	+236.2%
Car	$1,500	$24,072	$35,000	+45.4%
Gallon of Gasoline	16¢	$2.57	$2.33	-9.3%
Gallon of Milk	21¢	$3.37	$3.60	+6.8%
DC Comic Book	10¢	$1.60	$3.99	+149.4%

Groceries

Nutley Margarine (1lb ctn.)	16¢
White House Evaporated Milk (3 tall cans)	24¢
Kitchen Craft Flour (No.10 bag)	43¢
Pillsbury's Pancake Flour (40oz pkg.)	18¢
Wisconsin 2-Year-Old Cheese (per lb)	50¢
Snowflake Crackers (1lb box)	15¢
Jolly Time Popcorn (2x 10oz cans)	23¢
Nestle's Candy Bar (x2)	24¢
Sunnyfield Wheat Puffs (3x 4oz pkg.)	13¢
Nabisco Shredded Wheat (pkg.)	10¢
Fresh Ground Peanut Butter (2lb)	29¢
Prudence Corned Beef Hash (16oz can)	22¢
Libby's Chili Con Carne (2x No.1 cans)	23¢
B&M Baked Beans (28oz can)	16¢
Del Haven Cream Style Corn (No.2 can)	12¢
Ann Page Spaghetti (2x 15½oz cans)	13¢
Val Vita Tomatoes (3x No.2½ can)	25¢
Heinz Ketchup (2x 14oz bottles)	35¢
Ann Page Salad Dressing (quart jar)	34¢
French's Mustard (6oz jar)	9¢
Sweet Navel Oranges (3 dozen)	25¢
Rome Apples (4lb)	19¢
Sunsweet Prunes (2lb pkg.)	22¢
Sweet Potatoes (3lbs)	19¢
Carrots (3 bunches)	10¢
Round Bone Roast (per lb)	28¢
Sirloin Steak (per lb)	38¢
Lamb Leg (per lb)	29¢
Lamb Chops (per lb)	25¢
Loin End Pork Roast (per lb)	26¢
Sliced Bacon (per lb, no rind)	32¢
Pickled Pigs Feet (14oz jar)	21¢
Sliced Pork Liver (per lb)	25¢
Fresh Mexican Sea Bass (per lb)	28¢
Coldstream Pink Salmon (No.1 tall can)	17¢
Canterbury Tea (¼lb box)	15¢
Red Circle Coffee (2x 1lb bags)	45¢
Folger's Coffee (1lb can)	30¢
Del Monte Grapefruit Juice (2x No.2 cans)	15¢
Libby's Tomato Juice (2x No.2 cans)	17¢
Red Rock Cola	5¢
Camay Toilet Soap (3 bars)	20¢
Kleenex (440-sheet pkg.)	25¢
Scott Toilet Paper (x2)	15¢
Nature's Remedy All-Vegetable Laxative	10¢
Oxydol (giant size)	63¢
Kellogg's Ant Powder	10¢
Doyle's Dog Food (3x No.1 cans)	15¢

Clothes

Women's Clothing

Stept's Wallaby Coat	$35
Harris' Felt Hat	$1.89
Markell's Slack Suit	$2.99
Harris' Velvet Dress	$5.95
Marks Bros. Printed Silk Shantung Dress	$3.98
Stept's Sweater	$2.49
Markell's Plaid Skirt	$3.93
Warner Girdle	$7.47
Movie Star Lacy Slip	$1.29
Helene Of Hollywood Brassiere	$1.25
Penney's Rayon Panties	49¢
Quilted Ray Floral Print Robe	$6.93
Markell's Flannelette Pajamas	89¢
Red Cross Vagabond Shoes	$7.45

Men's Clothing

Harris' All-Wool Top Coat	$24.75
Markell's Men's Gabardine Jacket	$3.93
Stetson Straw Hat	$5
Harris' Single / Double Breasted Suit	$24.75
Sears All-Wool Sweater	$4.98
Towncraft De Luxe Shirt	$1.98
Smart Rayon Tie	49¢
Markell's Dress Slacks	$3.93
Penney's Rayon Robe	$4.98
Montgomery Ward Broadcloth Pajamas	$1.98
Jarman "Moc-San" Leather Shoes	$6.85
Everett Slippers	$2.98

Toys

Sears Streamlined Scooter	$2.82
Tiny Tots' Pedal Bike	$1.62
Carved Wood Hobby Horse	$9.69
Toyland Electric Freight Train	$13.88
Electric Portable Phonograph	$7.39
Gilbert 43-Piece Chemistry Set	$3.95
Colonial Type Dolls House	$2.29
Sears 18in Momma-Poppa Doll	$3.19
66-Piece Plastic Tea Set	$1.98
Boys' Cowboy Suit	$3.47
80-Piece Farm Set	$1.49
Slate Easel Blackboard	98¢
Sears Big-60 Game Box	93¢
Artificial Leather Football	$1.26
Ball & Basket Outfit	$2.46
Table Tennis Set	98¢

Other Items

Sonora Super 7 Static Free Radio	$53.50
GE Super 5 Golden Tone Radio	$26.50
Thermolux Super Automatic Water Heater	$59.50
Powermaster Food Mixer	$13.50
Waring Blender	$29.75
Olsen Jewelry Matched Engagement Set	$100
Gene Autry Flat Top Guitar	$6.95
King James Bible	$3.59
Parker Pen	$8.75
Tropical Seas Imported Rum (fifth)	$1.59
Mill Farm Whiskey (pint)	98¢
G&W Bandwagon Gin (fifth)	$1.33
Old Verdugo Sweet Wine (fifth)	27¢
Reno Club Pilsner Beer (12oz bottle)	5¢
Martinelli's Apple Cider (½ gallon glass)	39¢
Kools Cigarettes (ctn.)	$1.28
Habenella Doll Cigars (x5)	15¢
Cosmopolitan Magazine	25¢
Life Magazine	10¢

Money Conversion Table

Amount	1942	2021
Penny	1¢	16¢
Nickel	5¢	80¢
Dime	10¢	$1.60
Quarter Dollar	25¢	$4.01
Half Dollar	50¢	$8.02
Dollar	$1	$16.05
Two Dollars	$2	$32.10
Five Dollars	$5	$80.24
Ten Dollars	$10	$160.48
Twenty Dollars	$20	$320.96
Fifty Dollars	$50	$802.40
One Hundred Dollars	$100	$1604.80

(Cumulative rate of inflation: 1504.8%)

FOR VICTORY
BUY
UNITED
STATES
DEFENSE
BONDS
STAMPS

Where I work It's

CHESTERFIELD

Here's the answer to that.... Chesterfields are *Milder, Cooler-Smoking* and definitely *Better-Tasting* in just the way you want a good cigarette to be. And no question about it, there's a lot more smoking pleasure in Chesterfield's Right Combination of the world's best cigarette tobaccos.

For steady enjoyment, make your next pack Chesterfields... regardless of price, there is no better cigarette made today.

Chesterfields are on the job
with Smokers everywhere *They Satisfy*

U.S. Coins

Official Circulated U.S. Coins		Years Produced
Half-Cent	½¢	1792 - 1857
Cent (Penny)	1¢	1793 - Present
2-Cent	2¢	1864 - 1873
3-Cent	3¢	1851 - 1889
Half-Dime	5¢	1792 - 1873
Five Cent Nickel	5¢	1866 - Present
Dime	10¢	1792 - Present
20-Cent	20¢	1875 - 1878
Quarter	25¢	1796 - Present
Half Dollar	50¢	1794 - Present
Dollar Coin	$1	1794 - Present
Quarter Eagle	$2.50	1792 - 1929
Three-Dollar Piece	$3	1854 - 1889
Four-Dollar Piece	$4	1879 - 1880
Half Eagle	$5	1795 – 1929
Commemorative Half Eagle	$5	1980 - Present
Silver Eagle	$1	1986 - Present
Gold Eagle	$5	1986 - Present
Platinum Eagle	$10 - $100	1997 - Present
Double Eagle (Gold)	$20	1849 - 1933
Half Union	$50	1915

...for PROTECTION today
and PROGRESS tomorrow

Production for protection . . . production of aircraft — of all material of defense—at full capacity of men and machines. This is today's duty . . . the duty of all American industry—and of all Americans. This we do . . . whole-heartedly, 'round-the-clock.

And from today's intense experience will come progress . . . progress for the peace to come, and the protection of that peace. Out of the lessons of war . . . from warplane designs . . . will come new planes, greater planes, for the skyways of tomorrow.

LOOK TO *Lockheed* FOR LEADERSHIP *in both!*

LOCKHEED AIRCRAFT CORPORATION · BURBANK, CALIFORNIA

73

COMIC STRIPS

BRINGING UP FATHER

JUST KIDS

MUTT AND JEFF

THIMBLE THEARTRE STARRING POPEYE

Made in the USA
Monee, IL
27 August 2021